NEW YORK CITY: A BRIEF HISTORY

Second Edition

Robert R. Tomes
St. John's University

Custom Publishing

New York   Boston   San Francisco
London   Toronto   Sydney   Tokyo   Singapore   Madrid
Mexico City   Munich   Paris   Cape Town   Hong Kong   Montreal

Cover Art: Courtesy of PhotoDisc/Getty Images

Copyright © 2009, 2006 by Pearson Custom Publishing
All rights reserved.

Permission in writing must be obtained from the publisher before any part of this work may be reproduced or transmitted in any form or by any means, electronic or mechanical, including photocopying and recording, or by any information storage or retrieval system.

All trademarks, service marks, registered trademarks, and registered service marks are the property of their respective owners and are used herein for identification purposes only.

Printed in the United States of America

2009500059

MP

**Pearson
Custom Publishing
is a division of**

www.pearsonhighered.com

ISBN 10: 0-558-37270-8
ISBN 13: 978-0-558-37270-5

15 2020

CONTENTS

1	Dutch New Amsterdam, 1624–1664	1
2	British Colony	5
3	New York City During the American Revolution	11
4	A New City and A New Nation, 1783–1815	15
5	America's Economic Capital, 1815–1860	19
6	Tammany Hall and Boss Rule	25
7	New York During the Civil War	27
8	An Industrial Giant, 1865–1920	29
9	The Roaring Twenties	37
10	The Great Depression	39
11	World War II	43
12	Postwar Boom, 1945–1968	47
13	City of Crisis and Extremes, 1968–1992	53
14	Renewal and Challenge	57
About the Author		61

Preface

Few major topics of historical investigation have received as little attention as the history of New York City. One can find thousands of books written on hundreds of specific aspects of New York City's past, but only a handful of valiant authors have dared to treat the subject comprehensively. The reason is simple: The nature of New York City's history is so complex and so multilayered that any attempt to try to tell the "whole story" in one organized narrative account will almost surely disappoint. There are, in fact, three different histories of New York City, and most sane authors have chosen to address one of them at a time. First, New York City has a rich local history, which is a voluminous subject in itself. Local history automatically requires the service of great detectives because so much of the evidence comes from oral or legendary sources. Next comes another story—the story of how New York City became first the economic, and then, later, the cultural center of the United States of America. Finally, there is a third history—the story of New York City's place on the cutting edge of global change, as both creative innovator and leading participant in trends transforming the entire world. This brief account is a humble attempt to pick the key themes and events of each of these stories, and present them in a simple, straightforward way, so that the reader may gain a quick overview and establish a general context as to what, when, where, how, and why major events unfolded and how these influenced the city's cultural identity. No doubt many lovers of the "Big Apple" will be disappointed that more was not included, but my hope here is simple—to spark interest in this amazing and unique history, in the hope that readers will go on from here to examine further and discover for themselves the incredible richness of the incredible city known as New York.

I would like to thank my students and colleagues at St. John's University for all they have done to stimulate my interest and understanding of New York City. I express particular gratitude to Dr. Julie Upton and Dr. JoAnn Heaney Hunter for their inspiration and leadership in making New York City part of our core curriculum at St. John's. I gratefully acknowledge the hard work of Kim Yuster, Melissa Philbrook and Bruce Collin at Pearson Publishing for their roles in facilitating the development and completion of this project. Most of all, I would like to thank five native New Yorkers—Mary Quinlivan Tomes, my wife, and Christine, Claire, Kathleen, and Julie Ann Tomes, our four daughters, for all their interest, inspiration, and support. Any shortcomings or errors in this account are a result of my shortcomings, not theirs.

Robert R. Tomes
St. John's University
New York City

1

DUTCH NEW AMSTERDAM, 1624–1664

The Dutch were the first Europeans to establish a colony in New York. The Dutch built their empire in general, and their New World colony in particular, for the purpose of trade rather than overseas settlement. By the early seventeenth century, the Netherlands, despite being relatively small in size, resources, and population, had become one of Europe's wealthiest nations, and had a thriving merchant class when they set up the tiny colony which they named New Amsterdam in 1624. The Dutch made their biggest profits by trading sugar from the West Indies, spices and other agricultural commodities from Asia, and slaves from Africa. It was geography that primarily attracted them to New York. First, Henry Hudson, an explorer under Dutch contract, had vigorously promoted the potential of the vast harbor in which thousands of ships could find safety during the early 1600s. But strategic concerns contributed as well. The Dutch hoped to establish a base for trading operations in North America, where they lacked a vital presence. The Spanish had already settled Florida and California; the British, Virginia; and the French, Canada and Louisiana. New York was an ideal location, the Dutch reasoned, because of its proximity to both Northern Europe and the West Indies. Unlike the British colonies of Plymouth, Massachusetts Bay, Rhode Island, Connecticut, Pennsylvania, and Maryland, which were all established for religious reasons, New Amsterdam was founded for one reason only: to increase profit for the Dutch West India Company. From its very beginning, then, it is important to understand that money-making was central to the purpose and the cultural identity of the colony.

The fabled story of the Dutch purchase of Manhattan from the Indians for $24 is an exaggerated legend, as are most tales of Dutch New York traceable to Washington Irving's successful *History of New York*, written in the early 1820s. Manhattan was occupied by relatively peaceful Indians—the Leni Lenape, traders who hoped to gain from frequent contact with the Europeans. On the shores of northern Long Island (including present-day Queens), and along the Jersey Shore (near present-day Asbury Park), were more warlike tribes. The Dutch gave the Indians 600 guilders for Manhattan island—the equivalent of about a thousand dollars today, which is a little more than the legend, but still one of the best real estate deals in history. The key problem with the arrangement was that the Dutch understood the deal to be permanent, and the Indians thought it temporary. This set the stage for subsequent violence against the Indians by the settlers. This also established the pattern of excluding native Americans from the colony, rather than assimilating them, as the Spanish, Portuguese, and French were more likely to do in their own colonies.

The Dutch West India Company quickly built a fort on the present site of Battery Park, which served as a trading post. To encourage settlement, they gave out huge land grants to wealthy Dutch citizens to whom they gave the title "patroon." They hoped that these individuals and their families would create a social system in New Amsterdam that resembled Early Modern Europe—an essentially feudalistic structure in which a small aristocracy dominated a larger peasantry while small merchant and artisan classes made modest to comfortable livings. But the colony lost money at first, and there were better places in the Dutch empire to make a fortune. Desperate to encourage European settlers to come, and recognizing that they could not find enough of their own people to create a Dutch majority, the Company opened its doors to all Europeans. By the end of New Amsterdam's first decade of settlement, as many as fourteen European languages could be heard spoken daily on the streets of this tiny little settlement of only a few hundred, then a few thousand people. Perhaps the largest group was not even Dutch, but a community of French Huguenots who had been on the move seeking religious freedom to practice their unique form of Christianity. Thus, another hallmark of New York's cultural identity—diversity—also became part of its fabric of life from the very beginning, and clearly such early history played a critical and long-lasting role in its evolution. Before long, Jews, Catholics, and Muslims all came to the emerging colony. Faced with labor shortages, African slaves began arriving as well. New Amsterdam, like New York, never had one ethnic, religious, or racial group that could claim to be a majority of the population.

Two additional forces encouraged diversity in Dutch New York. First, because of its location at 40 degrees latitude, New York is centrally located on the North Atlantic. Not only did the Dutch trading post's amount of trade boom, its trade was significantly more diverse than the trade of other Atlantic ports. Places like Boston and Charles Town, South Carolina, became specialized ports early in their history. By contrast, New York's trade went to many more places, and the port began to serve as a hub, or point of exchange, where goods arriving from one place might only come there to be transferred to a different ship taking it elsewhere. This meant that merchant houses from all over the world would eventually open their doors in New York, making it a thriving center of international trade, in addition to its reputation for meeting local needs, like the fur trade, that developed from regional resources. A second feature encouraging diversity was the temporary and transient nature of many of its inhabitants. Unlike British colonies that were largely settled by families or people intending to build families, New Amsterdam was largely settled by young, unmarried men wanting to make money and move on elsewhere when that was accomplished. The result was yet another social experiment. Thus, taverns, gambling houses, and brothels were far more prominent in the community's early development than churches and schools.

After two decades, the colony had a growing reputation for sin and moral decadence, and failed to achieve profit margins consistent with high expectations. Frustrated, the Dutch sent a new governor, Peter Stuyvesant, to take over and clean things up in 1644. A tough disciplinarian, Stuyvesant quickly turned the colony around and set it on a path of economic success that it has never relinquished. During Stuyvesant's rule, which lasted until 1664, major improvements were made to the infrastructure of the city. A wall was built on the site of present day Wall Street, and all of Manhattan below that point was settled. A new fort was built, and bulkheads prevented the erosion of Manhattan. Docks were also built, and ferry service instituted to the surrounding regions of Brooklyn, Staten Island, Long Island, and Bronck's Farm, as well as Perth Amboy. A canal was built into downtown Manhattan, and a street that would become Broadway extended from the Battery to Wall Street. New Amsterdam's trade grew in leaps and bounds, with furs from the Hudson Valley contributing handsomely to growing profit margins. Before long, the Dutch rivaled the French for dominance in the lucrative North American Fur Trade. And trade ultimately brought another prominent feature to New Amsterdam: slavery.

2

BRITISH COLONY

In 1664, the British Navy sailed into the harbor and gave the Dutch Governor Peter Stuyvesant a simple ultimatum: submit to British rule or be destroyed by its artillery. Stuyvesant, inclined to fight, was forced to surrender by his colony's merchants, who saw no hope of resisting the might of British arms. Although the Dutch Navy would attempt to re-capture New Amsterdam in 1673, the colony was on its way to full membership in the British Empire, and its name would soon be changed to New York, in honor of the future King James II, then the Duke of York. At the time of the British takeover, the population of the city was only about 1,500 persons, most of whom spoke Dutch but were of Flemish, Waloon, French Huguenot, Swedish, Danish, and German extraction. Many of English and Scottish descent did business in the town as well, and the English language was often used, although less frequently than Dutch. The British adopted a benevolent posture toward the Dutch and, in an effort to earn their loyalty, allowed as many things to remain unchanged as possible. The transition from Dutch to British culture in the colony seems to have been gradual. Although Dutch New Yorkers accepted the use of English as the official language, they retained much of their ethnic and political particularism until the end of the colony's history at the completion of the American Revolution.

Although the population began to grow, particularly in the 1700s, the British had a hard time recruiting ethnic English subjects to come. Most of the English coming were single men who, like the Dutch, sought adventure and money-making before ultimately moving on to settle down elsewhere. To hold the colony against potential rivals, open immigration policies were enacted to attract settlers, regardless of their ethnic background or religious beliefs. The cultural result was profound: New York's ethnic diversity continued to become more and more differentiated, and the tiny but fast-growing city quickly became one of the most unusual and fascinating towns in the world, with its unique mix of people and cultures. Ethnic and religious diversity dramatically influenced the town's identity; for example, religious authorities, in this case the Church of England, the Official State Church, had far less authority here than in most places, simply because many in the community were not members. The disproportionate number of single men living in the town assured that it would continue to be known as a place where family-style institutions were often overshadowed by saloons, gambling dens, and brothels. New York sustained New Amsterdam's reputation as a wild town brimming with moral vice. Over time, British authorities did much to "clean things up," but the traditional sense of moral order that characterized other British colonies lagged behind here. Most of all, particularly among New York's upper merchant classes, earning money through trade became the common cause that drove society forward. The willingness and eagerness to pursue profitable business endeavors superceded many of the cultural divergences and tensions that the town displayed.

The British realized that the economic and strategic potential of the colony far exceeded what the Dutch were able to accomplish, and, in 1686, they undertook a major administrative reorganization by issuing a new charter. Brooklyn, Long Island, and Staten Island were reorganized into new counties, and renamed Kings, Queens, and Richmond respectively. The Royal Governor would have increased powers, and Thomas Dongan would receive a huge land grant in Staten Island for use as his personal estate. (Today this neighborhood is still called Dongan Hills). The Governor's conduct of affairs and policies would be assisted by a new council, consisting of a handful of the most powerful men in the colony, appointed by the King, and elections would be allowed to create a local assembly that would raise local taxes and legislate local matters, provided that it passed no laws contrary to the laws of England. All measures passed by this assembly technically had to be reviewed and approved by the Lord of Trade, later the Board of Trade—the King's appointed ministry in Britain that oversaw his colonies. Occasionally, conflicts developed, the most famous of which were the cases of Leisler's Rebellion and the Libel and Sedition Trial of John Peter Zenger. Leisler was a New Yorker of Dutch descent who attempted to form a government and once again align the colony with the Dutch when the Glorious Revolution occurred in 1688. He was convicted of treason and hanged. Zenger was a printer who published a newspaper that became critical of the authorities and official imperial policies during the 1730s. He was put on trial for treason and sedition, but was acquitted after a jury trial.

In general, New York politics during the British colonial period were best described as "factious," at least until the crisis that led to the American Revolution began to unfold in the 1760s. What this meant was that a small number of wealthy families and individuals dominated the local government, but depending on who the appointed governor happened to be, different groups or individuals could be "in" or "out" of the inner circle at any given time. These highly personalized politics often led to disputes that would spill over into newspaper and tavern discussions, but in reality were less serious than they may have appeared. Personal outcomes proved more significant than ideological beliefs in politics. As for the development of self-government in the colony, middle and lower class New Yorkers went to work, lived their lives, and had little input into public affairs. If anything made them more "free" than their European counterparts, it was the relative absence or diluted presence of traditional European institutions that exerted authority: monarchy, aristocracy, the Church, tradition, law and custom, and ethnic and religious homogeneity. And, most of all, many discovered the ever-present opportunity to make money. Despite occasional squabbles, life in British New York went on with little to suggest that a revolution would one day take place. Circumstances changed more quickly than anyone could have imagined when the Seven Years War ended in 1761.

In the 1700s, the economy of British America took off, and its population doubled every twenty five years. New York was in the forefront of this exponential growth. By the eve of the American Revolution in the 1760s, its population had risen to 15,000. The British Empire developed a sophisticated network of trading patterns, in which New York was ideally suited to assume a major role. Britain imported agricultural products from North America and the West Indies. They exported manufactured products to these same colonies. To protect and encourage the growth of British industry, the colonies were forbidden to produce most items manufactured in the mother country.

The Atlantic Slave Trade also figured prominently in profits. Most slaves were forcibly removed from coastal points in West Africa and transported to the West Indies, from where they were sent on to additional slave markets throughout the coastal towns of the Americas. New York had its own slave market, where imported human beings were held and auctioned off to traders and buyers. Most of the profits New York merchants made were not directly related to the slave trade, but, ultimately, the lavish economic success of the overall commercial system rested on the hideous institution. Ships transported Africans to the West Indies, where they exchanged their human cargoes for sugar, which in turn often came to New York, where sugar or molasses was then made into rum. When one examines the overall balances of exchange and profit, it is almost impossible to find anyone in the British commercial network who did not owe a good portion of their financial profit, even if indirectly, to slavery. After all, agriculture provided the base of new wealth created in the Americas, and what made agriculture profitable was in large part the fact that owners did not pay laborers' wages. Getting most of their real estate from Native Americans without paying for it helped, too! Imagine running any business without having to pay the people working for you? Imagine running a business built on property that you didn't have to buy or rent?

The Dutch West India Company had first imported slaves to the city in 1628. When the British took over, about 9% of the population was African. By the dawn of the American Revolution, the number and percentage of slaves had increased substantially: Over 3,000 Africans, constituting over 14% of the population, lived in Manhattan alone. Most of these Africans were slaves, although some were free. Most slaves served as domestic servants in the homes of New York's wealthiest families, but a large number worked as day laborers whose owners rented them out to perform various jobs. Some of these slaves eventually became artisans and skilled laborers, and European workers often complained that they provided stiff competition. Slavery in Colonial New York seems to have been filled with ambiguity and contradiction. New York slaves usually experienced deplorable living conditions, had no legal rights, and suffered numerous abuses, but they seem to have been able to experience more freedom than many of their counterparts employed in agriculture. Slaves in New York may have had more freedom of movement and right to assembly, thus enabling them a bit more freedom on which to build the foundations of community.

The growing importance of New York to the British Empire became clear during the Seven Years War, 1754–1761, known in the colonies as the French and Indian War. The French attempted to expand their Canadian Empire into the Great Lakes Region, and the British, unwilling to allow this, sent the largest military expeditionary force assembled up until that time in human history to stop them. At first, the war, which broke out near present-day Pittsburgh, went badly for the British, but it ended as a rather lopsided victory, after which the French were forced to give up Canada to Great Britain. The war transformed New York. Because most of the fighting happened in Canada, New York became Britain's supply base, and the Hudson Valley became a crucial corridor for military operations. The war turned New York into a virtual boom town, with many merchants making windfall profits. But the war's end brought a local recession to these same industries. Furthermore, heavily in debt from the cost of the war they had won, Parliament levied heavy taxes on the colonies, thus initiating the constitutional crisis that led to the American Revolution. Many New Yorkers served in the New York militia during the war, an experience that prepared many of them for the War for Independence which would follow. And most of all, the total defeat of the French changed New Yorkers' relationship to the mother country: no longer having a hostile foreign power as next-door neighbors, the colonists were less dependent on the British Army and Navy for protection. And finally, with the French gone, the rich territories of upstate New York occupied by Indians no longer supplied with French weapons now seemed ripe for settlement. In 1765, Parliament passed the Stamp Act, and New York exploded. The coming of the American Revolution had begun.

3

NEW YORK CITY DURING THE AMERICAN REVOLUTION

The British and the Patriots both considered New York City of critical importance the moment the War of the American Revolution began. The British figured that if they could occupy New York City and use the Hudson Valley as an avenue of attack from the south and the west, and their navy to control the ocean to the east, they could isolate the rebellion to New England, surround it, and eventually subdue it. George Washington understood immediately that if the British successfully occupied the city, the Southern and Middle Colonies would be separated from the Northern Colonies, potentially undermining the unity upon which the hope of the Revolutionary Cause rested. Although the war began in Massachusetts, as soon as Washington was appointed Commander-in-Chief of the Continental Army in 1775, he began to prepare for the defense of New York City as his top military priority. By the spring of 1776, Washington had committed most of his army and mustered local militias to the city, which the British attacked just as the Founding Fathers were about to sign the Declaration of Independence. In fact, in Philadelphia, the vote for independence was delayed as the Continental Congress learned that the British Navy had sailed into New York Harbor and might level the entire city with its awesome firepower. Perhaps as many as 80% of the city's inhabitants quickly fled once the ships were sited, even before military operations began. Not until the New York delegation courageously voted in favor of independence did the resolution in Philadelphia pass.

The British had a lopsided advantage in the battle that followed, because New York's waterways provided their Navy with a safe highway to transport troops and resources and to dispatch artillery around the region. The Patriots had no navy. The British first occupied sparsely settled Staten Island. Staten

Island was actually a Loyalist stronghold; in fact, the Reverend Samuel Seabury, Pastor of St. Andrew's Anglican Church, still thriving in present-day Richmondtown, was one of the most prominent and outspoken Loyalists in the colonies. Washington prepared for an attack that he anticipated would follow the logical path of today's Staten Island Ferry route. Patriot artillery was placed along Battery Park, Brooklyn Heights, and Governor's Island facing Staten Island. After the experience of the Battle of Bunker Hill, the British correctly assumed that a frontal attack would lead to many casualties, even though they dramatically outnumbered the Patriots. What followed, however, was not a speedy end to Washington and his army, but the beginning of one of the great "what ifs" of military history.

The British ferried their troops around Coney Island and landed in Gravesend Neck Bay, near present-day Sheepshead Bay, where they launched what was then called the Battle of Long Island. (Today we obviously refer to this as Brooklyn, not Long Island). Attacking the Patriots from their rear guard and advancing up a path close to where today's Coney Island and Flatbush Avenues run, the British systematically approached Brooklyn Heights, mechanically defeating wave after wave of Patriot forces that tried to rally a line of defense. By nightfall, Washington's army was encircled on Brooklyn Heights, and sunrise promised the final British assault from the East on land with their Navy behind Washington's back in the harbor below. In perhaps the greatest escape in military history, Washington evacuated his entire army in the middle of the night in dead silence across the East River, departing on barges from Brooklyn where the base of the Brooklyn Bridge stands today, and landing in Manhattan at Kips Bay, where NYU Medical Center is presently located (FDR Drive and 34th Street). Legends, folklore, rumor, and imagination have celebrated this event since it occurred. One story told how Patriot ladies entertained British commanding officers while Washington got away, and numerous armchair generals speculated that General Howe, in charge of the British forces, was possibly even a Patriot sympathizer, but the factual record supports little of this. Guerrilla tactics used by the Patriots in New England had exacted unprecedented casualty rates on British forces, who adapted by employing more conservative methods, which they hoped would ultimately favor their overwhelming superiority in numbers. Why rush when time is on your side? Additionally, credit has to be given where it is due—Washington's retreat exercised masterful deception, as well as remarkable precision and discipline. Keep in mind, Washington knew the environment well, and the small population that remained supported his cause wholeheartedly. The British at one point sent their Navy to sail up the Bronx River, in reality a tiny little brook on which ships could not sail, but the incorrect maps they possessed depicted it as a significant waterway.

The next morning, the British pursued the battle to Manhattan. Again Washington was forced to retreat north, up the path of present-day Broadway. He occupied the highest part of Manhattan, hoping to withstand another British assault. This site now bears his name—Washington Heights, and so too does the famous bridge that was later built there. Seeing how badly outnumbered he was, he retreated again, north into the countryside, eventually setting up headquarters at West Point.

The Battles of Long Island and New York were the darkest moments of George Washington's public life. For the remainder of the long war which followed, he daily dreamed of returning to New York City, which the British promptly occupied and turned into a huge base of operations for their forces throughout North America. The local population, except for a few Loyalist sympathizers, had fled. The British Navy used the harbor until the end of the war. After the British surrendered at Yorktown in 1781, New York momentarily became a ghost town. Many of the Loyalists who had flocked there fled with the British Navy, correctly assuming that many of them would be tried as traitors and their properties seized, now that the Patriots had won the war.

New York was so significant to Washington that when the British left New York City he returned to disband the Continental Army and give the famous Farewell Address to his troops in downtown Manhattan at Fraunces Tavern (still in operation as one of New York's most prestigious restaurants). Finally, six years later, when Washington was sworn in as the first President of the new United States of America he came to New York City, which was temporarily appointed as the first capital of the new United States of America. The inauguration took place on Wall Street, just a few feet away from the present-day New York Stock Exchange. (Today, you can visit the Federal Building National Monument, which still stands on this location. Admission is free, and it contains a museum dedicated to the event).

The Revolutionary War, in more ways than one, marked a dramatic end to the colonial town of New York, and a radical new beginning for today's city. First, on September 21, 1776, just a few weeks after the British had taken control, a great fire broke out. Four hundred and ninety-three homes, constituting one third of the buildings in Manhattan, were utterly destroyed. The entire city west of Broadway would have to be built again. Second, the Revolution led to a substantial turnover in political leaders. Many wealthy New Yorkers had cast their lots with the British, and hence were forced to flee with them. In many cases, their property was confiscated and distributed to Patriot soldiers as pay for their service. (One such grant was given to a young captain who had distinguished himself—Isaac Roosevelt. The land he received lay along the Hudson River at Hyde Park). But most of all, a new generation of leaders came to local power, bringing with them a radical new vision, spirit, energy, and plan for the future. Among them was a young man still in his late twenties, distinguished as one of the greatest heroes of the war: Alexander Hamilton.

4

A NEW CITY AND A NEW NATION, 1783–1815

The end of the War of the American Revolution brought a new beginning to the city in more ways than one, and it is no exaggeration to say that modern New York was born the day that the British Navy sailed out of the Narrows in 1783. Many Loyalists left with the British and, when the native population returned, the turnover in people was dramatic. Also, much of the city had to be rebuilt after the fire.

In short, the American Revolution accomplished two things: it changed New York City's circumstances, and it provided the city with a new generation of leaders. New York was no longer inhibited by the restrictions placed on it by the British Empire. Although it would take time to achieve its potential, New York was now on its way, building new and remodeling old institutions and practices. Economically, the city's merchants now faced a brave new world of limitless potential but frightening challenges—they could trade with new partners anywhere in the world—but now they lacked the British Navy's protection. And the departure of the British also meant the opening of new territories upstate New York, which would be catastrophic for Native Americans, but before long the region would become America's leading granary or "breadbasket." Wheat provided New York's merchants with a precious commodity to send to population centers elsewhere.

New York's Patriots of the Revolutionary Era quickly assumed leadership roles in national, state, and local politics. None of them would prove to be more important than Alexander Hamilton.

Alexander Hamilton was, in many ways, the quintessential New York success story. His vision, energy, and talent contributed greatly to defining New York's identity. Hamilton was born in the West Indies. He was considered an illegitimate child because his mother's first husband deserted her before she could obtain a legal divorce—almost impossible for a woman to do in those days anyway. She remarried later, and Hamilton was born to that nuclear family, but, due to her earlier situation, Alexander was considered a bastard and branded an outcast. His parents died when he was only a teenager, leaving him an orphan. All who knew him were struck by his intellectual brilliance, good looks, and likable personality. A wealthy merchant took a liking to him, allowed him to intern in his firm, and then gave him a scholarship to come to New York to study at King's College, (Columbia University) with the hope that someday Hamilton could run a New York office for the firm. Hamilton arrived in 1774. He quickly distinguished himself at school and joined the Revolutionary Movement. He soon joined the New York militia and fought so bravely in the Battle of New York that George Washington asked him to join his personal staff. Hamilton proved himself to be such a talented and hard worker that Washington had him write much of his personal correspondence. Hamilton became like an adopted son to the General. In the Battle of Yorktown, in which the British were finally defeated, Hamilton personally led the charge over the ramparts which led to the British surrender. Hamilton returned to New York a nationally renowned war hero, close personal friend of George Washington, and an insider to political inner circles of the New Nation. Hamilton quickly got to work back in the city. He established a successful law practice and plunged into public life. He also became a passionate opponent of slavery, and founded the New York Anti-Slavery League. He worked tirelessly toward this goal for the remainder of his life, and New York became one of the first states in the country to make the slave trade illegal in 1787. When the new constitution was proposed, Hamilton, seeing that a stronger national government would benefit New York, became one of its biggest promoters. He wrote most of the Federalist Papers to persuade public opinion to ratify the new government. New York became a key swing state in the ratification process, and Hamilton, along with another New Yorker, John Jay, was instrumental in the outcome.

When Washington was elected President, he chose Hamilton as his Secretary of the Treasury, and a strong case can be made that Hamilton was the most influential member of Washington's Cabinet. Whereas the American imagination tends to be more sympathetic to Hamilton's major political opponent, Thomas Jefferson, the Federalist agenda that laid the basis for America's economic success as a new nation was, for the most part, Hamilton's plan. As controversial as these policies were at the time, and as politically difficult as it was to obtain support for them, it is hard to imagine that the fledgling nation would have survived without them. This is particularly the case with Hamilton's insistence that a central bank and general debt be created, and that America develop its own manufactures rather than depending on Europe to produce goods. To gain Jefferson's support for policies based on these principles, Hamilton agreed that the permanent capital of the United States be established on the border of Virginia, present-day Washington, D.C. This fateful decision has had its advantages and disadvantages for New York over the years. It has given New York more freedom to emerge as a business and cultural center, not in the spotlight of competing national politics, but it has left the nation's most important city a political outsider on more than one occasion. Hamilton was a defender of cities and urban life, while Jefferson hated cities and believed that true gentlemen should reside on country estates. Hamilton felt a strong and active government was necessary to solve problems and mobilize resources, and in the end government could use its power to achieve humanitarian goals. Jefferson stated bluntly, "The government which governs least governs best." America eventually became a country modeled after Hamilton's vision more so than Jefferson's, and twenty years after his death, New York City had effectively taken its place, embodying Hamilton's plan in action.

New York City played a major role in the politics of the New Nation. During Washington's Presidency, it remained a Federalist stronghold, but the new democratic trends which swept the country after 1800 quickly made an impression in this rapidly developing city. From 1789 to 1812, the city's economy grew, but felt continuous stress from turbulence in Europe. First, the Wars of the French Revolution and then the Napoleonic Wars made Britain and France constant enemies from 1792 to 1815. This conflict quickly led to world war, and control of the seas became a constant bone of contention. New York as a seaport constantly had its commerce interrupted. In 1812, the United States was eventually drawn into the Napoleonic Wars, but when peace was finally secured in 1815, America in general and New York in particular would emerge with a new independence. The key to this would be economic independence; after 1815, Americans became determined to develop their own economic success that no longer relied on European manufactures, trade, and money. New York City was about to play the central role in the making of that American economic independence.

5

AMERICA'S ECONOMIC CAPITAL, 1815–1860

The end of the Napoleonic Wars marked the beginning of a new period in world history, in which unimagined growth in population, urbanization, industrial production, and global trade would take place. New York City was ideally situated to be on the cutting edge of this incredible change, and in the years that followed, New York would not only exemplify global trends but be a key player in developing them. Between 1815 and 1860, the city would become an economic giant. It would become America's largest city, the center of the new nation's financial and trading networks, and as such, the nation's economic capital city. Additional developments during these years would lay the foundation for the city to become the nation's cultural center, and develop its industrial capacity in the years after the Civil War. But the most celebrated aspect of New York City life during these years has been the arrival of millions of new immigrants from Europe, and the fascinating creation of new ethnic, urban, and political cultures their arrival stimulated.

One personality and two local political events at the beginning of this period would have as much influence on the subsequent history of New York City as any other. The person was Dewitt Clinton, and the two events were the building of the Erie Canal and the adoption of the grid system as a new map for Manhattan.

DeWitt Clinton was born in 1769 to a prominent New York family. His father was one of Washington's generals in the Revolutionary War, and figured prominently in the politics of the new state. During his long career in politics, DeWitt Clinton would serve multiple terms as mayor of New York City and Governor of New York State, as well as being a U.S. Senator and Presidential candidate. Clinton's politics were remarkably flexible—at different points in his career he was aligned with factions of differing ideological persuasion. He was immensely popular more often than not . Most of all, he was a visionary, a booster, a builder, and a promoter of economic growth and opportunity who dreamed of New York being the nation's economic nerve center.

Clinton's greatest personal achievement was his role in the building of the Erie Canal. Detractors called it "Clinton's Ditch," and even supporters were frightened by the enormous amount of money that had to be borrowed to complete the project. Governor Clinton secured the approval for the building of the canal, which began in 1817, and was completed in 1825. The canal stretched 363 miles from east to west, connecting the Hudson River to the Great Lakes (technically the Mohawk River to Lake Erie with several tiny local waterways incorporated). Despite its staggering cost of $7.8 million for locks alone, the project was an enormous success which quickly paid for itself and made considerable profit. Across the entire nation, a frenzy of canal building followed, which rarely duplicated New York's impressive success. The opening of the canal proved to be the most important formative event in the economic histories of New York City and State. Transportation routes pioneered by the canal would be reinforced decades later when railroads were built, and in the Twentieth Century when highways were built. Stated simply, the canal transformed geography by creating a transportation route for people and products from the Atlantic Ocean to the interior of the United States. Whereas America had numerous harbors along the Atlantic Coast, the Appalachian Mountains, of which the Catskills and Adirondacks are part, stretched from Maine to Georgia. Travel from the coast to rich agricultural heartland of the country was time-consuming and difficult for people, and almost impossible for commerce. Despite the agricultural potential of America's heartland, the simple fact was that farmers lacked the ability to transport products from most locations in the interior of the country to population centers along the eastern coast and in Europe, where they could be sold at great profit. The Erie Canal solved the problem. By linking the Hudson to the Great Lakes, cargoes of wheat and other agricultural products could be loaded on barges at western points along the waterway and shipped east, eventually reaching their destination in New York City. On the return trip, the barges could carry manufactured goods with high consumer demand to the isolated interior of the continent. New York City quickly became the gateway to North America, serving as the point of departure for exports, and the point of entry for imports. Before the opening of the canal, Philadelphia and Boston boasted larger trade than New York, but the human re-engineering of the geographic environment permanently changed that. New York quickly became the nation's busiest port, and one of the busiest harbors in the entire world. Soon, New York firms were pioneering new trade routes, extending their reach to the Pacific Ocean, the Mediterranean Sea, and all seaports along the Atlantic coast of Europe. New Yorkers seized the opportunity to invest profits in building new institutions and infrastructure. They transformed old economic institutions with innovations that would ultimately enhance their leadership of the American economic miracle.

DeWitt Clinton was also intimately connected with the development and execution of the "Grid Plan" for New York City, although his achievement in this was not as personal as it was in promoting the canal. Clinton obtained approval for the so-called "Commissioner's Plan" from the State Legislature in 1811. The plan created the orderly development of real estate in Manhattan from present-day 14th Street to Washington Heights. It designed Manhattan's avenues and numbered streets and parceled out its lots in standardized sizes. The plan assured sustained economic growth, and gave New York City its distinctive physical appearance. The grid system allows for light and wind to physically penetrate the island of Manhattan. No matter how tall the skyline, Manhattan is never dark during sunlight. No matter how many people may be on its streets, one is constantly aware of being outdoors, because its air circulates. The grid system also assured the human transformation of the physical geography of the land. Excepting Central Park, which would later be set aside, the hills and valleys of Manhattan would be leveled, its ponds and streams filled in, and a new unique urban geography, transformed by human intention, would be created.

Geography alone did not make New York's economic success inevitable. Individual New Yorkers did significant things to promote success. Between 1815 and 1860, many of the innovations that built the modern economy were first tried in New York. When it came to doing business, New Yorkers quickly developed a reputation for daring and experimentation; they paid less attention to established tradition and conventional practices, and the risks they took paid off handsomely. New York merchants changed the way commerce worked, and from the substantial profits they made, built America's investment banking system. The key to shipping, New Yorkers understood sooner than anybody else, was time. By developing innovations that moved goods more quickly, predictably, and efficiently, the port soon possessed unrivaled advantages over its competitors. Beginning with the institution of fixed shipping schedules in the 1820s, (up until then the ships stayed at the dock until they got filled up), and culminating with the laying of the Transatlantic cable, New York took the lead in changing the way business was done.

A key problem the world's merchants faced in the early 1800s involved money. Little currency was in circulation. Central banks either did not exist or were too limited in scope, and credit was difficult to obtain and in short supply. Out of the profits of trade, New Yorkers built the modern banking system, with the career of Moses Taylor providing a remarkable illustration. First credit, and then the development of investment capital, provided the key to the process. Moses Taylor began by trading Cuban sugar, went on to become a lender, and transformed banking by initiating competitive interest rates. By the end of his life, Taylor's portfolio had diversified into manufacturing, retail, and real estate, as well as commerce and banking, and his personal properties were dispersed around the country.

Another amazing New Yorker during this period was Alexander Stewart, whose career changed the history of retailing. He created a store which presaged the invention of the department store. Stewart started in clothing sales, but came up with a radical idea: make shopping a pleasurable experience. He tailored his store to women who had time and money to shop, but before long it just kept growing and growing because of its popular mass appeal. Modern retailing with New York City as its inspiration was on its way.

Immigration surged from the 1820s to 1860, when the Civil War broke out. During these years, most immigrants came from Northern and Central Europe. The British Isles were the biggest supplier. Many came from Scotland and England, but by the 1820s, the group which attracted the most attention were the Irish. The Irish were different, because they were Catholic and the others were Protestant. Today, tensions and differences among Christian groups are less pronounced than they were in the 19th century. The Irish often encountered nativist fears that the Pope was secretly plotting to overthrow or undermine the United States. Discrimination, prejudice, and violence soon followed. The legacy of the Irish as the first group that was different is still with us today: we all routinely refer to a resident alien's work permit as a "green card," even though it is not green, and we refer to the police vehicle that is used in making multiple arrests as a "paddy wagon," even though its transportees are not necessarily of Irish descent.

Most of the immigrants who came were relatively poor, and from rural areas where modernization and rising birth rates displaced millions of peasant farmers and sent them to cities in search of work. But two traumatic events in Europe unleashed millions in total desperation in the 1840s.

The Irish Potato Famine began in 1844 and lasted five years. In the spring of 1844, samples of potatoes, which served as the staple of the Irish diet, were observed to contain a fungal disease which turned them rotten while still in the ground. One of the worst crop failures and sagas of human devastation in known history was about to follow. When the famine started, the population of Ireland was over eight million people, but by 1849, it probably fell to about three and one half million. Half died of starvation and disease; half emigrated elsewhere. Some went to the booming industrial towns of Britain, like Liverpool and Manchester, some went to Australia, but the largest number poured into the Atlantic seaports of America, especially Boston and New York. The famine did not simply create a popular immigration trend—it was nothing less than a vast human crisis on a grand scale, having much in common with today's most desperate refugee crises. In many cases, Irish estates were owned by absentee British landlords, who found it cheaper to provide Atlantic passage to their starving tenants than food. The result was not authentic voluntary emigration, therefore, but entire communities being displaced more or less arbitrarily. If you were given a choice of staying where you are to face almost certain starvation, disease, guaranteed poverty, and likely death, or taking a boat ride to start new someplace else, what would you do? To those totally destitute, with no hope of a better life where they are, the exit plan obviously seemed the best choice. It came, however, with few assurances that the new life would be dramatically better than the old. Hundreds of thousands of "Famine Irish" began arriving in New York Harbor in the summer of 1846. So many of them were so sick by the time they arrived that a huge area along the Narrows in Staten Island was turned into a quarantine station. At least 100,000 died there. (For years, local historians had searched without success to locate the mass grave that contains their remains; but, in 2006, construction workers excavating in the former Baltimore and Ohio Railroad yards along the St. George waterfront, not far from the Staten Island Ferry Terminal, discovered the site.) Those fortunate enough to survive the trip then usually made their way to places elsewhere in the United States, or to the poorest neighborhoods in the city, where they hoped to find work. Five Points and the Bowery along Manhattan's Lower East Side became notorious slums containing high concentrations of these poor souls. Much has been said and written about the awful conditions in these immigrant slums, and most historical research confirms the enormous human price and suffering of the participants involved.

 The German States exploded next, detonated by the Revolutions of 1848. Another wave of destitute masses sailed to America, these very often motivated by political struggles, and fleeing the massive police crackdowns that followed the failed uprisings. In the years that followed, New York and America would not only receive millions of ethnic Germans, but would also come to be viewed as a safe haven from political oppression and a place to exercise personal freedom. Once again, the "Golden Door" opened. Once again, they came from abroad.

Ethnic New York was now officially a work in progress, with outcome unknown. Could so much diversity be tolerated? What do we know about religion, language, politics, and culture? Do not societies require adequate common ground to function properly? This was something new and untried. Would it work? Poverty, violence, political corruption, vice, crime, gangs, political and religious disputes—in short what old New Yorkers viewed as moral decadence—seemed everywhere, trying to reconcile itself with the economic colossus that was emerging. The City was a tinderbox of paradoxes and extremes, side by side, fully crammed into the same physical space. Would the forces of civilization prevail, or would social chaos and political anarchy follow?

6

TAMMANY HALL AND BOSS RULE

Three unique conditions contributed to rise of "Boss Rule" in New York City from 1830–1930: First, the spread of participatory popular democracy that mobilized the urban masses; second, the need for rapidly growing cities to construct modern infrastructures, such as transportation and water systems or police and fire departments; and third, the arrival of record numbers of immigrants, all seeking employment and in need of being assimilated. The most prominent feature of Boss Rule in American memory is the prominent corruption that came to characterize the political machines, but this was only one part of the story. Boss Rule may have made graft and bribery commonplace, but with vast amounts of money at stake, the system provided jobs for immigrants and assimilated many of them into the American political process. The bosses also provided a safety network in times of need—often giving out food and clothing during crises and providing help to some of those facing dire personal circumstances.

New York City had one of the most notorious political machines in America, and it was associated with the Democratic Party for nearly a century. The machine's headquarters were eventually located in the infamous Tammany Hall, located at Union Square, (16th Street and Third Avenue to be exact). The organization began as a political club, formed in 1788 to give artisans and craftsmen a chance to express themselves, as these groups were not always welcomed in the inner circles of the Federalist and later Whig Parties that were dominated by the city's wealthiest citizens. The original name of the association was the Society of St. Tammany, derived from the Delaware Indian Chief known as Tamanend, whose image became the symbol and later official insignia of the group. The association's fortunes became tied to the rise of the Democratic Party in the 1820s. Martin Van Buren, a New Yorker, Andrew Jackson's Vice President (1828–1836) and principal political strategist, played a key role in making the Democratic Party the party of urban immigrants. New immigrants became the urban voter base of the party, and to assure turnout and loyalty, Democrats provided jobs, patronage, and other support.

In New York, the machine evolved in the 1830s to become an enormous organization, permeating the city's life and greatly influencing its political identity. The huge number of public works projects, and the vast human service needs of building a modern city, provided prizes that the bosses cherished. The city was divided into wards, based upon the geography of voting districts. Each district had its own chain of command, with a boss on top. Often the rank and file came from groups of men who belonged to volunteer fire departments. Taverns and saloons played an important role in political life, as members and lieutenants often gathered on a regular basis at predictable locales, (not unlike how today's football pools work). Saloons were often named after or owned by major players in the neighborhood structure, like Patrick Kelly and Matthew Brennan of Five Points, the notorious 6th Ward. Meanwhile, the tribal alignment of these districts created a central leadership that commanded the Party throughout the City, eventually building the site at Union Square for its headquarters. A series of colorful characters occupied the central command position in the 19th century, most infamous among them Fernando Wood (1812–1881), William M. "Boss" Tweed (1823–1878) and "Honest" John Kelly 1822–1886). Tweed built an empire that eventually stretched to state government and private industry. Tweed's fortunes rose through contracting and kickbacks, but he was able to monopolize city purchasing. Thomas Nast exposed Tweed's corruption in a series of the most famous political cartoons in American history, but years passed before the "Tweed Ring" was finally deposed, tried, convicted, and imprisoned in the 1870s. With the help of political allies, Tweed actually jumped bail while on prison leave, and traveled around the world before being caught and returned to the United States! Although the mid-19th century displayed the peak of boss rule, the legacy lasted until the election of 1932, when a series of corruption scandals and the Stock Market Crash finally brought down Mayor Jimmy Walker and the local Democratic Party with him. This paved the way for Fiorello LaGuardia, an outsider and a reformer, to be elected Mayor and begin cleaning things up.

7

NEW YORK DURING THE CIVIL WAR

New Yorkers were divided at the outbreak of the Civil War. As was the case throughout the Northern States, most New Yorkers felt that slavery was wrong, but questioned the value of going to war to end it. New York's wealthy merchants and bankers at first feared that war would disrupt business: the lucrative cotton trade that they financed would come to a sudden stop. And what if Southern States and cotton farmers defaulted on millions of dollars of outstanding loans that they owed New York bankers? Poor New Yorkers were concerned also: if the war ended slavery, might the freed slaves leave the South and head North to compete for jobs, particularly at the lower end of the wage scale? Despite these ambiguities, once the war began, the antislavery position became more popular than not, and by 1864 the cause of abolishing slavery had genuine mass appeal.

The war proved to be a turning point in New York's history, which quickly became inseparable from the Union's cause. The Federal Government, desperate for credit, turned to New York's bankers to finance the war. And most of all, the war dramatically stimulated New York City's manufacturing sector. The war assured that New York would become an industrial giant for the next century, making its manufactures almost as significant as its commerce and its banking on a national scale. When the war ended, New York's industrial society was an established fact, and would dominate the city's social and cultural life for another hundred years. With this boom came all the exaggerated extremes of the factory system: vast wealth and new investment capital on the high end; massive social problems and human suffering on the low.

Much has been written, both at that time and since, about the notoriety of the infamous New York City Draft Riots of 1863. Only a few years ago, Martin Scorcese popularized these riots in the movie *Gangs of New York*. Some have argued that the riots revealed massive popular resentment against the war on the part the working class and immigrants, while others have used the episode as a measure of lawlessness and gang violence in the city at the time. The movie, and many similar accounts, unequivocally exaggerate the actual events, which were in reality quite complex, filled with political ambiguity, and most likely had more to do with internal conflicts among competing local factions in the gangs than common opposition to the Civil War. Authorities were caught off guard by the riots, whose outbreak seemed remarkably spontaneous. The city's National Guard units, a visible component of any major 19th century city's public safety team, had been sent to Gettysburg to brace for Lee's attack. All in the city were stunned by how quickly the riots spread, and how violent they became, though riots and gang violence were not uncommon in the poor and working class sections of New York City in the 1840s and 1850s. In fact, many of these, usually triggered by elections, were far worse in the number of injuries and property destruction than the riots of 1863. What significantly differed about the 1863 riots was that the warring factions left their own territories on the Lower East Side and assaulted uptown areas where people with money lived. The traveling mobs targeted wealthy abolitionists and pro-war newspaper editors and businessmen. The police were overwhelmed, and the National Guard units dispatched to Gettysburg had to be recalled to the city. After several days, tranquility was restored, and immediately investigations began to sort out what happened. One of the great riddles in New York history is how many people were actually killed. Eyewitnesses honestly believed that thousands of people must have died, but when all was said and done, the most liberal accounting procedures could yield only 120 deaths, and, in all likelihood, the actual number was probably between 30 and 40, most of whom perished as depicted in the movie—through inter-gang violence, not political protest or police brutality. The incident made a deep impression on the outlook of New Yorkers, and anxiety over urban unrest remained intense for the remainder of the 19th century.

8

AN INDUSTRIAL GIANT, 1865-1920

The end of the Civil War brought an industrial boom to the city which made its local economy the financial nerve center of the nation and a pioneering leader in new global economic trends. As the number of factories in the city grew, waves of immigrants poured in from Europe each year, and the city's African American and Asian populations surged, all to meet labor needs. The factories made money, and money translated into capital. New industrial sectors in transportation and energy emerged, requiring formation and investment capital at levels never previously imagined. In the 1850s, railroad building would herald the coming of a new age in banking. And the trend toward huge conglomerates and vast credit supplies was effectively stimulated by the Civil War, creating a new economic environment. New York's importance as the center of America's financial and commercial networks continued to increase, and rapid growth, with its dramatic extremes of wealth and poverty, reached greater levels. The late 1800s are generally considered a period of enormous human suffering, in which the problems of rapid, unplanned urban development reached truly frightening proportions. But the Progressive Movement launched in the beginning of the 1900s is often credited with, if not ending the social ills of the Industrial Revolution, at least beginning the process of political reform and social welfare that for the first time made the city a more livable place.

As the 19th century ended, the urban environment in any of the world's large industrial cities faced standard problems: inadequate and unsafe housing; lack of transportation systems; public health epidemics caused by inadequate water and sanitation systems; unstable employment conditions and lack of safety in factories; limited or nonexistent services in health care and education; political corruption; domestic and gang violence; vice; crime; alcoholism; conflicts among immigrant groups; and, finally, the fact that anyone unable to support themselves, such as widows, the elderly, the disabled, or orphaned children, faced life on the outer margins of society. In short, the combination of poverty and the lack of a social welfare net guaranteed that the human cost of economic success would be great. New York City had its share of these problems, and the arrival of numerous ethnic and racial groups maximized tensions. Just as New York was in the lead of developing social ills, so it would also play a key role in addressing them. Ultimately, economic growth enabled more and more New Yorkers to enter the mainstream of American economic life, and the city developed the institutional infrastructure to begin coping with these problems.

Immigration patterns changed after the Civil War, and most observers began calling it the "New Immigration." Before the Civil War, most immigrants came from Northern Europe, and with the exception of the Irish and a small number of Bavarians, were Protestant. After the Civil War, patterns shifted to include southern and eastern Europe. Most of the immigrants arriving between 1880 and 1920 were Catholic or Jewish. American New Yorkers seem to have been distinctly less comfortable with this shift, and wave after wave of nativists resentment was launched against them. Everywhere, ethnic and racial tensions seemed to be on the rise, and some nativists, such as Madison Grant, a Professor at Columbia University, preached theories and wrote books that displayed outright racism. Despite the hardships immigrants faced, however, they kept coming. Why? Probably because despite all they had to endure, conditions were still better here than they were in the places that many of them left. And despite the cries of hatred against them, labor needs remained high.

Extensive demographic research has attempted to answer the key questions about economic opportunity for these new immigrants. Was the American dream a reality or a myth? How many went from "rags to riches," and how many died in virtual poverty? Did they all stay, or did many eventually return? Did different groups achieve assimilation and economic success more quickly than others? Historians have been able to render fairly reliable aggregate data for many of these questions; others will forever remain in the realm of speculation, because they entail value judgments. We can confidently say that it was possible but unusual for immigrants to arrive penniless and become extremely wealthy. And we can say that new arrivals came with relative strengths and weaknesses. Many Jews, for example, were already cosmopolitan people in Europe, with significant percentages having a high level of education and some financial resources in pocket. It would prove easier for them to adapt to the urban environment than it would for landless peasants arriving from rural areas. If it was unusual to go "from rags to riches," it was not unusual to make a living and build a better life, and this more than anything else probably explains the overall success of the New York experience. Through hard work you might not become rich, but by the end of your life, you would often be better off than when you started. Most of all, your children had a real chance of a better life than you had, which may not have been possible in your homeland. Social mobility rates among the various groups have been studied extensively, most notably in Thomas Kessner's *The Golden Door*. It seems fairly safe to say that Jews, particularly in their second generation, moved up quicker than all other groups, with Italians a close second behind them. The reason why is also very statistically clear: these groups more than any other emphasized the need to educate their children. The Irish lagged behind all European groups, but here the reasons are less clear. Many have pointed out that many of the Irish immigrants did not come by choice, and were displaced by the numerous crises of internal 19th century Irish history, such as the Great Potato Famine of 1844–1849. As a result, more of them had fewer resources and greater difficulty adjusting. Another variable also skews Irish mobility statistics is that when the Irish were able to educate their young, many of these success stories entered the clergy of the Catholic Church, becoming priests and nuns rather than money-earning professionals. African Americans suffered relentlessly. Segregation, discrimination, and racism overshadow all aggregate data for economic success for these New Yorkers, who would not begin to take their place in the upper economic layers of New York society in proportional numbers until the late 20th century. Much these days is said about assimilation and bi or multi-lingualism. Here again, history reveals a different story than myth. Not all immigrants came to stay, and hence they embraced American culture with varying degrees of enthusiasm. Almost all immigrants who came as families stayed, but many Italians and many more Greeks came as single men, worked, and returned.

As much as the Statue of Liberty, a gift from the government of France, erected in the New York Harbor in 1886 to celebrate the friendship between the two nations, came to symbolize the story of these millions of immigrants, the same period was also known for a group of larger than life personalities who also left an indelible imprint on the identity of the city: the Robber Barons. Some, like Andrew Carnegie, arrived as penniless immigrants. (Carnegie, like Bill Gates, would at one point become the richest man in the world). Others, like Cornelius Vanderbilt, grew up inauspiciously in Staten Island. Love them or hate them, and few are lukewarm to them, Carnegie, Vanderbilt, John Jacob Astor, John D. Rockefeller, Alexander Stewart, and J.P.

Morgan all transformed the economy of the United States, and each figured prominently in the local history of the city. As the Lower East Side and Hell's Kitchen brimmed with tenements, mansion after mansion was built along Fifth, Madison, and Park Avenues to accommodate the new generation of millionaires, magnates who had made their fortunes in monopolizing new sectors of the economy: Carnegie made his money in steel, Rockefeller in oil; Vanderbilt, Gould, Frick, and others in railroads, Stewart in retail and finance, and, ultimately, Morgan in investment banking. Committed to a philosophy called "Social Darwinism," these men thrived on lopsided success achieved through cutthroat economic competition, which they viewed as producing a healthy "survival of the fittest." They built America's financial and corporate engine and placed New York City in the driver's seat. And when they achieved success beyond their wildest expectations, they became philanthropists whose gifts were responsible for the founding of so many of the city's cultural institutions built during these years: the New York Public Library, the American Museum of Natural History, the Metropolitan Museum of Art, Carnegie Hall, just to mention a few. Conspicuous wealth and its lavish display remain imbedded in the city's culture today, hand in hand, side by side with the story of those who have as little at the opposite end of the economic ladder.

None of these "Captains of Industry" could exceed John Pierpont Morgan in importance. Morgan's father had been a banker and an instrumental player in the City's early years of assuming importance as the nation's banker. In the years following the Civil War, young J.P. took the family bank and transformed it into a global powerhouse, extending its operations throughout Europe and playing a growing role in financing the United States Federal Government in the days before the Federal Banking system we now have was created. Wall Street became important before the Civil War to raise money for railroad construction, and it had saved the Union during the Civil War by financing the war. As important as these developments were, New York's true financial clout did not become apparent until the final decades of the 19th century.

Modern American popular culture also began to develop in the city during these years. This was the era of vaudeville and the beginning of Broadway. Spectator sports became a growing interest, with boxing and baseball in the lead. In short, more New Yorkers were making enough money to begin to spend on leisure and recreational activities. The 1920s would bring about a dramatic increase in how many could.

During this period, the physical geography of the city changed a great deal. First came the making of Central Park, a major triumph for improving the quality of life in the city.

Wealthy citizens proposed the building of a park, and the plan submitted by Frederick Law Olmstead was approved in 1853. Over the next decade, an arduous reconstruction of the physical environment created a new institution unlike any in America. In an age of stratification, the park became a place for all New Yorkers.

Other landmarks to be built in the late 1800s included Grand Central Station, the Brooklyn Bridge, Carnegie Hall, Museums of Art and Natural History, and the New York Public Library.

But no building project would transform the city more than the creation of its subway system. First came the "El" train, so called because it was elevated. Then came subways. The city's water systems were also improved. Bridges, roads, and public buildings sprung up in numerous locations. Boss Rule and political corruption went hand in hand with these projects, but so too did the employment of immigrant masses to perform the labor.

Improvements in the city's transportation infrastructure profoundly changed the city's relationship to the world, the nation, and surrounding and nearby counties. Furthermore, new transportation systems had a profound social impact, transforming the ways in which New Yorkers came into contact with each other on a daily basis. Finally, the massive scope of these projects would come to have significant economic, political, and cultural implications.

New York's railroad system was initially limited by geography. Connecting the island of Manhattan to the mainland proved a gargantuan challenge. Cornelius Vanderbilt, the nation's mightiest railroad tycoon in the 1850s, quickly established a monopoly of rail connections into the city. His New York Central entered New York City from the Hudson Valley through the Bronx. These lines would later evolve to become today's Metro North rail line. By 1859, once a few small tunnels and bridges were built, trains could enter Manhattan and terminate at the site of present-day Grand Central Station at 42nd Street. Vanderbilt used his enormous wealth to buy political influence so that he could maintain his monopoly into the beginning of the 20th Century.

He was also aided by geography. Whereas as Vanderbilt's competitors, primarily the Pennsylvania Railroad, sought a route into Manhattan as well, the Hudson River proved too mighty an obstacle for them, and their lines were forced to terminate along the New Jersey side of the river. Thousands of people crossed the Hudson daily on ferry boats to complete their journey to Manhattan. The first attempt to build a railroad tunnel under the Hudson, launched by Colonel Haskins in 1873, failed miserably, as numerous accidents

An Industrial Giant 33

and overwhelming cost doomed the project. (Eventually it was completed and became the tunnel used by PATH trains). Next, a dream of building a railroad bridge across the river similarly failed. Finally, in 1901, Alexander Cassatt, the president of the Pennsylvania Railroad, developed an innovative plan, inspired by new technological developments. A vast underground tunnel could in fact work, he believed, if the trains running through it were powered by electricity instead of steam. And the tunnel could be safely embanked in the riverbed if it was anchored to the bedrock beneath the river by pylons. This tunnel would be much deeper, and be constructed as an "underground bridge," thus preventing it from shifting from the movement of silt or the weight of the trains. Built at a staggering cost, the new system was completed with the opening of Pennsylvania Station in 1911. The railroad tunnel system contained two tunnels under the Hudson, and four under the East River. Two of the East River tunnels connected Pennsylvania Station to the Long Island Railroad, and two of them linked to Sunnyside, Queens, where additional rail yards were set up. Finally, plans were made for the building of the Hell's Gate Railroad Bridge, which was not actually completed until 1935. This final link would connect to New England's rail networks.

These links were important for several major and noteworthy reasons. First, Manhattan was finally connected directly to the network of rail lines in the South and the Midwest, which had previously been outside of Vanderbilt's grip. This greatly enhanced New York City's economic ability to compete both nationally and globally as a viable commercial center. Next, the rail links also transformed the areas surrounding the city, making them accessible to a host of commuter lines and increasing urban sprawl.

The new City Charter of 1898 formally consolidated the five boroughs. Improved public transportation was the plan's main attraction for the residents of Brooklyn, Queens, and the Bronx. The City had originally contracted with three separate private companies to build reliable subway lines. Back in 1868, the first modern mass transport rail system had been introduced to Manhattan: the Elevated Manhattan Railroad, known as the "el" train. Four lines ran a north/south axis through Manhattan at 9th, 6th, 3rd and 2nd Avenues. Only the Second Avenue "el" extended all into the Bronx. None of the lines extended to Queens or Brooklyn. The elevated system reduced street congestion, but it also provided many drawbacks. The biggest was that steam power was both dirty and noisy, so real estate values along the lines quickly depressed, and neighborhoods in close proximity, for example "The Tenderloin" (24th to 42nd Streets between Sixth and Seventh Avenues) became seedbeds of vice and social hardship.

The subway would travel underground in Manhattan, be powered by electricity and its lines would extend throughout the Bronx, Queens and Brooklyn. The first subway line, the Interborough Rapid Transit, (IRT), operated by August Belmont, opened in 1904. The Brooklyn-Manhattan Transit (BMT) lines opened in the 1920s, and the Independent (IND) line in 1932. During these years, the IRT was also substantially expanded.

The building of the subway was a cumbersome undertaking in a busy city like New York, as streets had to be closed while the construction took place, and many wondered if cost would ultimately exceed benefits. Doubters were quickly proven wrong as the "Nickel Ride" (five cent fare regardless of the distance traveled) became an immediate success. New York City quickly became, and continues to remain, the largest, most complex, and most modernized mass transit system of any city in the world. In the 1930s, the private companies were officially consolidated, and a new public transit authority was launched by the LaGuardia Administration. The Subway had three dramatic effects on New York City: first, by maintaining a minimal fare of five cents for decades, the subways brought New Yorkers of all classes and categories together in a diverse cross-cultural interaction never seen before in the human urban experience. New Yorkers of all walks of life rode side by side in the same subway cars day in, day out. Neighborhoods of distinctive identity were now linked by but a few minutes travel time. Regardless of occupation, New Yorkers now traveled to work together. Second, the subway system revolutionized the economy of the city, making it far more efficient and opening its potential for growth. And, perhaps most of all, it revolutionized the housing market by opening up the Bronx, Queens, and Brooklyn as viable residential areas.

All of these changes to the infrastructure were so great that a major change in municipal government occurred in 1898: The current city of New York, consisting of the five boroughs, was created by a new charter. Up until then, New York and Brooklyn were separate cities, with Queens gravitating toward Brooklyn, the Bronx toward Manhattan, and tiny Staten Island on its own. The general terms of the agreement featured the building of mass transit lines across the East River and throughout Brooklyn and Queens, in exchange for Brooklyn agreeing to renounce its political autonomy and join the new consolidated municipal entity. As the new century began, New York was literally a new city, taking on the physical dimensions it now has for the first time.

One global event and one local event had extraordinary influence on the city at the end of this period: the Triangle Shirtwaist Fire of 1911, and the onset of World War I, 1914–1918.

An Industrial Giant 35

The former broke out in a clothing factory in Greenwich Village on March 25, 1911. In less than fifteen minutes, 146 women had died. Investigators were awestruck by the conditions which they discovered on the site, and the suffering of those who worked in this horrid sweatshop. Newspaper after newspaper reported one sordid detail after another, until public outrage reached fever pitch. Few local events left such a deep impression on public opinion. Finally, in response, New York City's leaders mobilized to attack the worst evils of the Industrial Revolution, and the process of creating the building and workplace safety codes and regulations that we now have was begun.

World War I began the process that World War II would complete in redistributing power around the world. In 1914, Europe was the economic and cultural center of the world; by 1945, it would be neither. The political landscapes of Asia, Africa, and the Middle East would pass through chaos, as nation after nation was born out of the dissolution of European Empires. This global process would have a major influence on New York's history, and provide the immediate setting for the "Roaring Twenties."

9

THE ROARING TWENTIES

World War I stimulated the financial, commercial, and industrial base of New York City's economy in new and expansive ways. Few people realized at the time, however, how dramatically World War I would transform the city's global role. After war broke out in Europe, New York banks with insurance guarantees backed by the American Federal government began lending money to the Allied powers, whose debt surged to meet war expenses. By the end of the war, France, and more so, Great Britain, had borrowed billions of dollars from New York banks. And Europe lay in economic ruin, due to the tremendous destruction the war had caused. Again, to finance recovery, Europeans would continue borrowing vast amounts of money from New York banks. (One may draw some interesting parallels here: For the past three years, the United States has been borrowing vast amounts of money from Asian banks to finance the Wars in Iraq and Afghanistan, as well as the tax cuts passed by the Bush Administration. What do the long-term results of this debt threaten to be?) The American Government, determined to promote economic stability and peace in Europe, guaranteed these recovery loans through the Young Plan and the Dawes Plan in the 1920s. Although it received very little attention at the time, just as today's transfers to Asian banks receive very little attention, the world's banking center shifted from European capitals to New York, and Wall Street assumed the prestigious and critical place that it currently holds in the global economy today. Fifty years later, when the city's industrial base would collapse as factories closed or moved elsewhere, the city would remain an economic giant in large part because of the importance of its banking and financial institutions.

The banking boom contributed to the rapid development of the city's skyline in the 1920s and 1930s, as numerous financial institutions involved in the formation and deployment of investment capital came to dominate the business culture. The Empire State and Chrysler (now Seagrams) Buildings were among those built. With growth came jobs in general and professional jobs in particular that required a more skilled or more educated labor force. New wealth poured into the city, the rich became even richer, and thousands joined the growing middle class each year. The city's new transportation lines facilitated the rapid development of residential neighborhoods in the Bronx, Brooklyn, and northern Manhattan. (Queens grew rapidly after World War II ended, and Staten Island after the Verrazano Bridge was built in 1964.)

The image most people have of New York City after World War I is very different and much more exciting: a place where modern popular culture was born and displayed some of its most dazzling features. New York City became the center of the Jazz Age, as Louis Armstrong, Duke Ellington, Billie Holliday, Ella Fitzgerald, Charlie Parker and countless others came to Harlem to perform at the Apollo Theatre and numerous other concert halls, theatres, dance halls, cabarets, and night clubs around town. Babe Ruth, newly traded to the New York Yankees from the Boston Red Sox, arrived just in time for the opening of the new Yankee Stadium. Spectator sports would enter the modern era. (Significantly, the controversy about the stadium was not its cost, but its location: after all, the Bronx was just starting to grow to its present size, and many asked, "Who would bother going all the way up there just to see a baseball game?") In Harlem, a group of brilliant African American poets, playwrights, and novelists led by Countee Cullen and Langston Hughes launched a literary and cultural movement called the Harlem Renaissance, a source of pride and measure of accomplishment for all African Americans. Downtown, F. Scott Fitzgerald wrote *The Great Gatsby* as Thomas Wolfe, John Dos Passos, Eugene O'Neill, and numerous other American writers visited or moved to Greenwich Village. New York soon became the nation's literary capital, and its local publishing industry boomed. By the 1930s, almost all of America's largest and most prestigious publishing houses were located in the city. Broadway assumed its modern importance in the city's theatre district. New York City took on a new role that would influence American and global culture: that of trendsetter, pacemaker, and innovator. Closely tied to this would be the city's ongoing role in retailing, advertising, and marketing revolutions, shaping modern consumer culture. As the nation's consumer economy developed, much of its identity would be defined in New York. Madison and Park Avenue were becoming as influential to advertising, and Seventh Avenue was becoming as influential to fashion as Wall Street had become to banking.

10

THE GREAT DEPRESSION

The Great Depression jolted New York City more than any event or trend that had preceded it. One of the myths that many Americans erroneously believe is that the infamous Stock Market Crash of 1929 caused the Great Depression. It did not "cause" the depression, although it was indeed a major component. The origins of the depression were international, and rooted in Europe at the end of World War I. Too much economic devastation, too much debt (even on the part of the war's winners) too much instability, and too many economic sectors and geographic regions, particularly in southern and eastern Europe, never really recovered from the war. To paraphrase an old saying, Europe was "struggling along on borrowed money and peace was on borrowed time." The Great Depression, therefore, which came to New York in October 1929, had been raging in parts of Europe for 12 years. Europe's dependence on New York banks proved catastrophic, and when Wall Street ran out of lending money, the national and global economies plunged into the greatest economic crisis of the modern era.

The big crash in October was preceded by two serious problems that went unnoticed: first, at the end of the summer of 1929, inventories stockpiled and factory orders dropped to a standstill—not enough people had enough money or purchasing power to continue buying consumer goods at the record pace that had been set during the boom years of the Roaring Twenties. Second, many stockholders owned stocks that they purchased "on margin." This meant that if you wanted to buy stock but did not have the cash up front, you could put the stock you already owned up as collateral to borrow against the purchase of new stock. This worked a little bit like taking out a home equity loan today. When the profits rolled in, you simply paid off the debt. The hidden problem was, what would happen if stock prices dropped? Imagine borrowing $400 for something that was suddenly worth only $200, and your back-up also collapsed in value? Everyone was lured into a false sense of security by the boom and upward trend of prices in the Twenties, but what would happen if a panic set in? That's exactly what happened in October—as people started to sell, prices dropped, and panic selling followed. Hoping to get back as much as they could, stockholders "dumped" their shares, and a sell-off took place, with prices in a free fall. Furthermore, because so much debt was redeemable in overrated or junk stock that now lost its value, creditors had little or nothing left to collect when defaults occurred. Fortunes were lost, and the world system of raising credit and investment capital became paralyzed, and was unable to fully recover for over a decade. Banking was only one sector of the world economy affected. Industrial production slowed, commerce and trade slowed, and, in addition to all this, an agricultural crisis had developed by the end of World War I with overproduction, debt, and purchasing power all being parts of the complicated problem. Hard times had come.

Hundreds of thousands of New Yorkers lost their jobs, and for millions of others, work became an on and off activity. Unable to pay rent and buy food, many became homeless. The West Side of Manhattan along the Hudson River became known as "Hooverville" named after the President—hundreds of thousands of "squatters" who had lost their homes or been evicted from their apartments camped out, making today's homeless population in the city seem miniscule in comparison. Soup kitchens and breadlines popped up all over town as a largely volunteer effort, often headed by churches attempting to give out free food and shelter to the needy. But all they gave still fell short; the need was enormous. Families broke up, and homeless children could been seen selling apples and newspapers everywhere. When Franklin Roosevelt was elected president in 1932 and launched the New Deal the following year, some of the suffering was alleviated, but New York continued to struggle mightily, and it was not until 1940 that the local economy recovered.

"The only thing we have to fear is fear itself," claimed the new President in his inaugural address in 1933. Franklin Roosevelt was a New Yorker, and the political ideas which he would bring to Washington and the coalition which he was about to assemble could have had their origin in only one place in the United States of America: New York. With its human diversity and economic complexity, with its political preference for pragmatism over ideology, with its common ground of economic opportunity, and, finally, with its location in the driver's seat of change, only New York politics could have prepared Roosevelt to be the President he would become.

The Depression transformed New York's position in American politics for the next four decades. New York quickly became the largest liberal state, with the city being its nerve center. New York would be to the Democratic Party what Texas now is to the Republican Party—not only a political stronghold, but a nerve center, a trendmaker, a source of ideas and values. New Deal public works projects transformed the face of the city as highways, tunnels, bridges, courthouses, post offices, schools, courthouses, and parks were all built or improved with Federal monies spent to put the unemployed masses back to work. The legacy for New York City's infrastructure would prove exponentially greater than the millions of dollars actually spent.

Few mayors of New York City had as much impact on its public life as Fiorello H. LaGuardia, who served from 1934 to 1945. Born on the Lower East Side of Manhattan to immigrant parents, his father was a free-thinking Italian Republican, and his mother a Hungarian Jew. LaGuardia's formative years were spent on military bases in the West and South, as his father was a U.S. Army commissioned officer and bandleader. The "Little Flower," as he became known (which is the English translation of Fiorello) was himself an accomplished coronetist and lifelong devotee of classical music, opera, and the arts in general. (One of his accomplishments as mayor was to establish the first public High School of Performing Arts in the United States, which is now a nationally recognized institution which bears his name and is part of Lincoln Center).

LaGuardia returned to New York City first as an immigration officer on Ellis Island, and later became a lawyer who worked tirelessly for numerous labor and immigrant causes. He subsequently entered politics, and was elected to Congress as a maverick Republican in 1916. Although LaGuardia never received the enthusiastic endorsement of the Republican Party, he was tolerated mainly because of the perception that it would be difficult to position a winning candidate in heavily Democratic territory. When the United States entered World War I, he enlisted and became a pilot. His exploits in Italy both as an aviator and an outspoken American commentator on war-related matters quickly gained national attention. After the war, LaGuardia returned to New York, and eventually ran successfully for mayor in 1933.

Fiorello LaGuardia was an independent Republican in a Democratic town. He opposed Tammany Hall throughout his career, and his election itself was made possible largely by huge scandals that brought down the previous administration of Mayor "Gentleman Jimmy" Walker. As mayor, LaGuardia's main goals were to break the power of Tammany Hall and the political corruption associated with it; to launch a full-scale war on organized crime and the huge networks of vice that festered from the alliance of police corruption and gang power; and, of course, to lead the city successfully through the crisis of the Great Depression. It was often pointed out in 1933 that the only elected official in the United States who was responsible for more employees and a larger payroll than the mayor of New York City was the president of the United States.

LaGuardia's crusades against political machines, police corruption, and gangs achieved moderate but incomplete success. The repeal of Prohibition also played a major role in breaking the power of the gangs. LaGuardia's personal flair proved quite unique. An immensely popular mayor, he both craved and received the public spotlight repeatedly. He enthusiastically embraced an endless stream of worthy public causes. In addition, he hosted a weekly radio program and was usually on the scene any time an important event developed anywhere in the city. Unpredictable and independent, few political leaders were willing to risk getting too close to him, and the end result was that when he retired at the conclusion of his third term, he left no machinery in place to carry on his ideas.

11

WORLD WAR II

World War II stimulated New York's economy unlike anything had before. Once again, the city's geography would prove critical. Because of its location relative to Europe, and because its natural borders made it easy to defend, New York Harbor became the port of debarkation for the millions of soldiers and trillions of tons of material which needed to be shipped to Europe to defeat Nazi Germany. The Battle of the North Atlantic raged up to the coast of Sandy Hook, New Jersey, just beyond the entrance to the harbor, but by 1942, the tide of success had turned in favor of the Allies. Convoy after convoy sailed out through the Narrows, as the docks of the city, from Staten Island to the Bronx, teemed with jeeps, tanks, trucks, weapons, and all things needed for the war effort. When the war ended, the convoys returned to the harbor, bringing many of the 25 million Americans who had served their country in war past a welcome and meaningful sight—the Statue of Liberty.

This boom unleashed the final phase of industrial greatness that the Northeastern United States would experience. The exhilarating impact of the war would stimulate the city's economy for another twenty-five years before decline finally set in. World War II also unleashed many important new social trends in the city. Ethnic particularism, for example, declined in the face of the common cause. African Americans in New York experienced the biggest economic leap in the history of their community, as the surging economic needs of war opened new and better opportunities for them. When the war ended, they would not relinquish their improved status and higher expectations.

The wartime economic boom also stimulated significant social and cultural change. Restrictive immigration laws passed by Congress in the 1920s, followed by the economic crises of the 1930s, reduced immigration levels to the city to its all time low. Industrial production for the war effort increased the demand for labor. With the Golden Door to the World closed, hundreds of thousands of African Americans from Southern States, and Latinos from Puerto Rico, migrated to New York City, lured by the dream of a better life and the hope of lucrative jobs in the factories, rail yards, and shipyards. Whereas some of them did in fact find successful employment, many were disappointed. New arrivals to the city had a long history of pain and struggle, as they tended to enter at the lowers steps of the economic ladder and fight their way up gradually over generations. Like many European immigrants before them, African Americans and Latinos were largely agricultural people, and experienced considerable shock migrating to urban environments. But white American prejudice against African Americans and Latinos was far greater than prejudice against Europeans, and many of the new migrants were surprised to discover that the city which had proclaimed itself a safe haven for freedom and harbor to the oppressed of the world, proved less idealistic in embracing racial minorities of its own nation. African American civil rights leaders quickly drew connections between the struggle for freedom abroad and the struggle for freedom for African Americans at home. Expectations on all sides rose. On the local level, tensions flared to the boiling point. In the summer of 1943, a white police officer probably used excessive force in arresting three African Americans at the Braddock Hotel in Manhattan. Rumors quickly spread that the police had killed the African Americans involved in the incident. Within hours, rioting, looting, and arson erupted in the Manhattan neighborhoods uptown where most of the city's African Americans lived. The riots lasted several days, and, for the most part, the rioters inflicted pain on their own neighborhoods and a small number of white merchants who owned shops in them. When things finally settled down, officials and the Press were hard pressed to refer to it merely as a riot and not a "race riot," but, in fact, that was misleading. In many ways, New York City had become known as a place wherein African Americans could do things that they simply could not do in other parts of the United States. But the painful reality was that freedom and toleration even in New York had its substantial limits in 1943. Even standing in the shadows of the Statue of Liberty, African Americans would have no easy walk to freedom ahead. Racial tensions would continue to escalate for decades, and African Americans and Latinos would face years of economic challenge fighting their way into the middle class. Indeed, to this day, they still remain overrepresented in lower income brackets. Disturbing patterns of housing segregation within the city emerged. Neighborhoods inhabited by African Americans and Latinos seemed excessively plagued by whatever social ills swept the city. And in the

1940s, for the first time, the Police Department and the criminal justice system seemed to be at the center of problems related to race.

The end of the war officially transformed New York City into an international city by making it the home of the United Nations. The complex of new buildings, erected on East 42nd Street, became the home of the new international organization designed to promote world peace and progress. Its history has proved a combination of success and failure, but its presence in New York would assure the continuance of the city's international importance. With the United Nations came diplomatic activity, international economics, and humanitarian concerns. New York has made significant contributions to progress in each area.

12

POSTWAR BOOM, 1945-1968

The United States experienced the largest and longest economic boom in recorded human history between 1940 and 1968. New York City would be on the cutting edge of America's success during these years, and the face of the city would be transformed by a wave of building and expansion that would give it its current appearance.

At the center of New York's economic importance remained banking, commerce, and manufacturing. But advertising, publishing, and retail would also soar to new importance. Broadcasting and communications would diversify and become prominent as well. As the skyline expanded and reached higher and higher into the sky, one new service industry after another made its appearance in New York. The local economy thus became less reliant on manufacturing for jobs.

One of the most controversial New Yorkers of all time, Robert Moses, would figure prominently in city history during these years. Moses, who played various roles in different government and quasi-public agencies, proved a pivotal player in both planning and executing the vast new public works projects that transformed the physical environment of the city and its surrounding environs. These projects aimed to accommodate the needs of New York's growing population, provide critical additional building space for industry and homes, and, of unforeseen importance, upgrade and expand the capabilities of the city's transportation system. During these years, new construction transformed the appearance of the New York City skyline, culminating in the completion of the World Trade Center in 1970. The system of highways, bridges, and tunnels which we have today was completed—the final phase for the opening of the 1964-65 World's Fair in Flushing Meadows.

(Shea Stadium and Forest Hills Tennis Stadium were built just in time for the opening of the Fair). The final sprawl of residential neighborhoods through the remainder of the five boroughs also took place. Queens, largely underdeveloped in 1945, took off at record speed, and Staten Island followed from 1965 to the present. The population of Queens nearly doubled between 1940 and 1960. The population of Staten Island has nearly tripled between 1964, when President Lyndon Johnson cut the ribbon at the opening ceremonies of the Verrazano Bridge, and today.

No public figure exerted a greater influence on New York City in the 20th Century than Robert Moses. None has left a greater legacy, yet few are as controversial. Moses, a native of New Haven, Connecticut, and a graduate of Yale University's Class of 1909, entered public affairs as an idealistic public servant committed to efficiency, modernization, and urban improvement. His biographer, Robert Caro, aptly characterized his ambitious career as a growing obsession with the acquisition and exercise of power. Two substantial areas of controversy regarding Moses persist to the present day: first, those associated with the man himself, and the methods he employed to achieve his ends; and, second, those relating to his accomplishments themselves—namely the vast system of public works which continue to bear his personal imprint due to the nature of choices and priorities that were his vision. Both are equally significant, and useful in that they can significantly inform our view of civic affairs in our own time.

Moses the man took on numerous roles in his long career, often simultaneously. This was one method Roman emperors often employed to increase their power. Moses was an expert in legal circumvention, who successfully evaded rules designed to prevent multiple office-holding and conflicts of interest. During the key period of 1945–1954, he served as the City's Commissioner of Parks, Coordinator of Construction, and Head of the City Planning Commission. He was also the Chairman of the Triborough Authority which controlled the Triborough Bridge and Tunnel Authority, a quasi-public agency with enormous financial clout resulting from toll collection and bond issuance. He also held a variety of titles under New York State auspices as well. From his entrance into New York City government as a reformer appointed by Fiorello LaGuardia in 1934, Moses quickly gained control of the city's public works as well as city initiatives launched by Franklin Roosevelt's New Deal. He remained a political force stronger than any mayor, governor or even president who would attempt to disagree with him or oppose him, until 1968.

Moses acquired dictatorial and autocratic control of these projects through a variety of ruthless methods. Like Senator Joseph McCarthy, the notorious communist witch-hunter, he would not hesitate to publicly humiliate an opponent, even on baseless charges, and, like J. Edgar Hoover, the secretive FBI Director, he maintained personal vendettas and systematically crushed anyone who disagreed with him publicly. This effectively bypassed the democratic decision-making process, and effectively made public works Moses' works. Moses' supporters, however, point out that although this was true, he still stands alone as the only person who was able to "get anything done." The concept that New York City was virtually "ungovernable" is easy to support when one looks at the long history of mayoral administrations, whether they were reformist or machine, that had approached the issues of transportation, housing, and infrastructure over the years without much success. Moses built the RFK Triborough, Whitestone, Throgs Neck, Henry Hudson, and Verrazano-Narrows Bridges. He also built the Brooklyn-Queens, Gowanus, Prospect, Staten Island, Van Wyck, Long Island, Clearview, Whitestone, Cross Bronx, Sheridan, Bruckner, and Major Deegan Expressways, as well as the Grand Central and Belt Parkways. He built more than 150,000 new apartment dwellings under Federal Housing auspices, and more than 1,000 apartment buildings under the New York City Housing Department. He also built the United Nations Complex, and most of the public buildings that remain in Flushing Meadows from two World's Fairs. Few individuals were ever as responsible for as much money, as many important projects, and as many jobs, as he.

Yet the legacy of Robert Moses continues to rest on controversy. Moses envisioned a future in which the automobile provided the main means of daily transportation. He thus built the highway and parkway system of the City and its surrounding counties to the exclusion of public transportation systems. Both commercial and private rail and water transportation systems declined significantly as a result. In the 1960s, the port of New York collapsed, losing hundreds of thousands of jobs and billions of dollars of business to other ports that had modernized to container shipping and were more accessible to interstate highways and rail lines. Moses was correct in predicting the increase of road traffic, but incorrect in predicting how much it would increase. Inevitably the system of roads he designed proved incapable of handling the eventual volume of traffic that it would need to accommodate. The highways often cut through residential neighborhoods in the city where hundreds of thousands of people forced were out of their homes to make way for the roads. The highways also stimulated suburbanization and encouraged middle class flight from the five boroughs. Moses' record in housing is also questioned. He bulldozed whole neighborhoods to make way for new construction. In some cases, such as the building of Lincoln Center on Manhattan's Upper West Side, gentrification followed, but in many others, high concentrations of spartan public housing developments, designed intentionally for people of low income, created neighborhoods filled with social problems and astronomical crime rates. If one views New York City as a city of extremes, Moses certainly contributed to pushing the margins of extremity further apart.

International immigration to New York City during these years reached an all time low, because Congress had passed restrictive immigration laws in the 1920s and reinforced these laws in the 1950s. Not only were numbers low, identity patterns changed little, because the laws established quota systems based on national origin. These laws unambiguously favored certain groups over others. So where did the growing population come from? Three sources: First, the Baby Boom. America's population soared, making up for time lost during the Depression and World War II. Second, large numbers of African Americans began to leave the depressed agricultural regions of the Southern States, and move to big cities in the Northeast and Midwest. Many came to New York. And finally, many Latinos began to move to the city, most of them during the 1950s and 1960s from Puerto Rico.

While New Yorkers were enjoying economic success on a spectacular scale, and boasting some of their greatest cultural achievements ever, new forces were silently at work undermining many of the roots of this success. The future held unseen challenges that would threaten the well-being and survival of the life of all of America's great cities. In 1956, the United States Congress passed a law which created relatively little controversy at the time, but which would prove in the long run to be one of the four or five most influential laws of the 20th Century: The National Highway Act of 1956. With Robert Moses playing a major role, New York City's roads, bridges, and tunnels were quickly connected to a new system of highways that extended into Long Island, Upstate New York, and New Jersey. The Long Island Expressway, Northern Parkway, Southern Parkway, Garden State Parkway, New York State Thruway, and New Jersey Turnpike were all either built from scratch or dramatically expanded. Highway construction unleashed the first round of suburban sprawl to transform the life of American cities. By the late 1950s, many towns just outside the City's borders in Nassau and Westchester Counties and Northern New Jersey were transformed from farmland into wealthy bedroom communities of New York City. Further beyond these towns, in areas further from the city, the highways connected people to brand new developments that offered affordable housing to the middle class. Levittown became a symbol of 1950s America, with a new showcasing of the American Dream in which the average guy could own a home, a car and a barbecue grill. At first, few observers would appreciate what would follow, but by the 1970s, the results would be staggering. Millions of middle class citizens would flee the city to take up residence in these new suburban communities, and the result for the big cities was life-threatening.

However, the Postwar period indeed marked a cultural highpoint for the city. World War II and the Cold War sent a tidal wave of European intellectuals, scientists, and artists scrambling to the United States as political refugees. Many of them, like Arturo Toscanini, the famed conductor who came to Riverdale, ended up in New York. The city not only became an international haven, but it continued its role as the leading American cultural city in a grander way than ever. Artists flocked to New York, which became the world's center for the production of modern art. Leonard Bernstein moved to town, wrote West Side Story, and became the Principal Conductor and Director of the New York Philharmonic. Bernstein soon became America's most famous classical musician. The Metropolitan Opera, long the most famous Opera House in the Western Hemisphere, moved into a new facility at Lincoln Center, where a huge complex of theatres, concert halls, libraries, and conservatories would rival or surpass the cultural facilities of any city anywhere in the world. Broadway thrived. Writers filled coffee shops and bookstores from the Village to Washington Heights, and New York City's universities witnessed astronomical growth in their numbers of faculty and students. New York City, long respected, now stood in the undisputed lead of the nation's, and indeed the world's, high culture.

13

CITY OF CRISIS AND EXTREMES, 1968–1992

The 1970s were the second worst decade of the city's history in the 20th century, and, in some ways, one of the worst in its overall history. The story, however, is not a simple tale of misery and decline; it is a story of ups and downs, winners and losers, and most of all, a period of extremes. Two national and international trends beyond New York's control threatened the city's economy from the mid 1960s to the mid 1990s: first, loss of jobs, mainly in industry, as American factories lost out to global competition elsewhere, and second, the flight of middle class workers to remote suburban areas. Today, manufacturing constitutes a minimal percentage of New York's economy, and a spectacular percentage of New York's workforce commutes to the city daily from surrounding communities. These two forces were critical in fostering the troubled events of the city's history during these years.

The crises began in the 1960s. Tension-filled riots erupted over festering racial grievances. Strikes and labor disputes paralyzed the city at times, the most famous of which shut down the public school system and later the transportation system. Power blackouts took place. Crime rates soared. Numerous residential neighborhoods within the city collapsed, and received the deplorable labels "slum," "inner city," or "ghetto." Apartment buildings designed to provide low-income housing for the neediest New Yorkers became frightening strongholds of crime, violence, and drug-trafficking. As social problems conspicuously plagued lower income groups in the city, middle income wage earners fled in ever greater numbers. As real estate values collapsed in declining neighborhoods, they surged in those with fewer problems. New York was daily becoming a city of extremes, where the rich lived in unprecedented luxury, but the poor suffered under conditions as unpleasant as those of the Industrial Revolution, and the middle class remained embattled. It reached its breaking point in 1975 and 1976: the municipal government of the City of New York reached the threshold of bankruptcy, and its financial operations were taken over by a newly formed quasi-state-run governing board. The city was forced to lay off tens of thousands of workers, and cut millions of dollars in public services. New York's social welfare net, which had experienced uninterrupted growth since the beginning of the century, seemed on the verge of collapse. The homeless population skyrocketed, and social ills mushroomed.

Political tensions of this period erupted on numerous occasions during the controversial mayoralty of John V. Lindsay (1966–1973). Lindsay from the beginning failed to fit any of the traditional molds common to New York municipal politics. Few political careers began with such promise; few ended in such disappointment. An articulate and attractive young man, whom many compared to President John F. Kennedy, Lindsay came from an old and wealthy New York family and had graduated from Yale University and Yale Law School when he successfully ran for Congress in 1958. Lindsay was a Republican, but an extremely liberal one, and he was a White Anglo-Saxon Protestant in the arena of New York's ethnic and racial politics. His first term as Mayor began with a devastating transit strike and subsequent years featured numerous prominent strikes, the most divisive of which involved the public school system. This aristocrat would side with New York's poor in battle after battle in the end only to be accused of raising expectations and making promises that could not be kept. At each step along the way, he made more political enemies among the middle class.

To ease significant cultural tensions of the day, Linday's main political goals of the day were to decentralize the public school system; to create Civilian Complaint Boards and render the Police Department more responsive to neighborhoods they served; and to consolidate municipal agencies more effectively, so that they would be more directly accountable to the mayor and less influenced by Tammany Hall. The first two goals were of pressing importance to many leaders of the City's minority groups. Lindsay also embraced many of the liberal suggestions offered by the Ford Foundation, a think tank which studied the city's problems carefully and concluded that community governance and neighborhood empowerment had to be substantially increased. Unfortunately, the merit of many of these liberal ideas will never be correctly assessed because the financial base on which they rested quickly collapsed. To pay for labor gains made by strikes, Lindsay called for a City income tax but it was hardly enough to pay the bills. Deficit spending ran its course quickly forcing the city to bankruptcy in 1975. In theory it may have been a feasible proposal to solve problems on a community level, but in reality, communities lacked sufficient resources to effectively get the job done. Power struggles for leadership positions in local communities also generated unexpected friction and often increased tensions. With jobs related to the Port of New York and manufacturing disappearing daily, and taxes being raised significantly, an exodus of middle class wage-earners leaving took place from the city.

In the end, the decentralization policies may have actually exacerbated the tendency of neighborhoods to become more rigorously defined by income status and racial characteristics than by healthy integration. How much all of this can be blamed on Lindsay personally is also questionable. New York was hardly alone in experiencing these problems suggesting that much larger forces were at work. Between 1968 and 1982 every major city in the Northeast and Midwest experienced similar problems. Thus the nation's cities and particularly its big cities all endured devastating times, the result of which were two profound demographic shifts: First the United States ceased being an urban nation and became a suburban one instead; and second, the population center shifted from the "Rust Belt" to the "Sun Belt". John Lindsay, community school boards and police review boards alone could not possibly have accounted for or caused these immense shifts ot take place.

One of New York's greatest achievements, the ability of its diverse peoples to live together amicably, faced new challenges as racial tensions reached heightened proportions. Race and poverty have a long and deep connection in American history. Racism, discrimination, and segregation extend far beyond the dominions of 19th century slavery, and New York City was no exception. In New York City, African Americans experienced a confusing group of paradoxes during these years. On the one hand, the city's liberal political disposition and traditions of diversity and openness offered its African American residents many more opportunities and considerably more acceptance than many other parts of the United States. But, segregation in housing and education remained an uncontestable fact. African Americans remained dramatically overrepresented in lower income status. And the schools to which many of them sent their children disintegrated into disgrace. Crime, as well as many other social ills, plagued the city's African American community in disproportionately higher percentages than white areas. New York's growing Latino population faced many of these problems and frustrations as well. Liberal good intentions had the adverse impact of raising expectations in the 1960s, and then subsequently anger, resentment, and disillusionment set in in the 1970s when the economic umbrella of success shrunk. Intergroup conflicts surged. Jews and blacks, formally one of the strongest alliances in local politics, turned on each other in outright hatred on numerous occasions. Anger flared everywhere, and by the 1980s, the term "culture wars" was an apt description of the city's local politics, with its hottest flashpoints becoming the public school and the criminal justice systems.

How bad did things get? The United States Census of 1980 recorded the first and only decline in New York City's population since the British Navy and Army occupied the city in 1776.

14

RENEWAL AND CHALLENGE

New York City's economy recovered gradually and unevenly after 1982. Its harbor and railway system had collapsed beyond recovery, and its manufacturing base had all but disappeared. But Wall Street enjoyed two spectacular rallies from 1983–1987, and from 1994–2000, bringing lots of money and business to the city. New technologies and global expansion led to new and often spectacular growth in New York's communications, advertising, retailing, and marketing industries. New York's acceptance of cultural diversity, and its traditional willingness to experiment and innovate, assured that the city would remain a favorable environment in which to do business. The nation and the world embarked on a new credit revolution in the 1980s, and the city, with its vast financial networks, was able get its fair share of profit. Economically, New York's financial institutions remain as important as ever. Hotel and tourist industries boomed in the 1990s, as did building and home construction. Economic recovery and change benefited many, though clearly not all, New Yorkers.

New York's African American and Latino populations have also undergone tremendous change since the 1980s. Both have displayed paradoxical trends in social mobility. Members of both communities have conspicuously taken their place in the highest places in American society. Colin Powell, former Secretary of State, for example, is a native of Harlem. And more African Americans and Latinos have entered the middle class than ever before. Educational statistics reveal the accomplishment of significant advancement for both groups from elementary to graduate study. Patterns of housing segregation are less pronounced, and discrimination in the workplace is now illegal. But despite these impressive gains, both groups remain overrepresented in the city's lower income groups and more troubled residential neighborhoods.

The population of the city has also changed dramatically. Beginning in the 1980s, a new age of immigration would begin that would rival the great ages of past immigration. The 2000 Census indicated that one out of seven New Yorkers was born outside the United States and immigrated here. Staggering percentages of New Yorkers speak languages other than English at home. And the patterns of immigration are very different: Europe, which in past times was the continent from which the largest numbers of immigrants came, today is last (excluding Australia and Antarctica). Most immigrants today come from Asia or the Americas, and significant numbers come from Africa. And the continental patterns reveal more diversity of homeland than ever. Immigration has also transformed New York's African American and Latino populations. The arrival of millions from countries like Haiti, the Dominican Republic, Mexico, Jamaica, and Nigeria have dramatically altered the composition of New York's minority groups. Asian Americans have further transformed the meaning of the term "minority" in New York City. These new immigration patterns have also transformed the religious identity of New York. Muslims and Buddhists have become the largest growing religious groups in the city. Latinos, Philippinos, and Vietnamese immigrants have maintained the Catholic populations of Manhattan, the Bronx, and Staten Island, but the percentage of the Catholics in Queens, and particularly Brooklyn, has plummeted. These immigrants have formed new communities, filled labor needs, and rebuilt and transformed numerous neighborhoods. Queens is now the most diverse county in the entire United States, and St. John's University main campus, located in Queens, one of the most diverse universities in the world. Some of the neighborhoods that experienced decline in the 1960s and 1970s have been reborn as new ethnic centers for these new arrivals. Gentrification has taken place in others close to subway lines and the business areas of Manhattan. But many sections of the city remain in great need of renewal, filled with poverty and desperation and inhabited by those for whom the American Dream has remained elusive. Many social scientists express concern that two types of poverty exist in New York: Temporary or generational poverty, which mainly effects newcomers, and permanent poverty, into which people are born and rarely escape. Optimists boast that the city's violent crime rates have reached all time lows, but pessimists remind them that the incarcerated population has grown exponentially, again containing disproportionate percentages of the poor and African Americans. Whereas New York has always been a city of extremes, it has always had its voices of dissent to condemn those extremes. Today's cultural environment may have fewer of those dissenters.

New York's cultural institutions bounced back from the Seventies, and some thrive more than ever. Tourism to the city increased exponentially in the 1990s, and the hotel industry has been one of the biggest growth sectors of the local economy over the past two decades. From Broadway to Lincoln Center to Yankee Stadium to Madison Square Garden, each year more New Yorkers and visitors have attended a growing number of cultural events. The present age reveals that more New Yorkers continue to be born elsewhere, and move here, reflecting the city's desirability. And many of the problems of the city's poor are at least indirectly tied to the fact that real estate prices have reached all-time highs.

On September 11, 2001, the darkest day in the city's long history took place. A group of terrorists hijacked two domestic airliners and crashed them into the World Trade Center, causing the Twin Towers to burn and collapse. Over two thousand New Yorkers died and many more were seriously injured on that day. Within hours, the world's communication airwaves were filled with proclamations that a new age in human history had begun. In the weeks, months, and years to follow, New Yorkers gasped at the scope of destruction incurred by the attacks and rallied heroically to recover and rebuild from them. Many have wondered if their traditional ways of life would be changed permanently as a result. Others feared that future attacks of similar nature could not prevented. But one fact remained undisputed: Just as the attackers chose their targets for their symbolic value, the people of New York proved more determined than ever to reassert these values that have always been at the heart of the New York experience. For them, the city's rebirth and recovery would be a statement to the world that the spirit of another New York symbol, the Statue of Liberty, has lost none of its power.

ABOUT THE AUTHOR

Robert R. Tomes is a native of New York City. He is Professor of History and Coordinator of Discover New York Programs at St. John's University in Queens. He earned his doctorate in History at New York University and his professional diploma in Education Administration at the City College of New York. He is the author of *Apocalypse Then: American Intellectuals and the Vietnam War, 1954–1975* and with Irwin Unger the co-author of *American Issues*, a two-volume documentary history of the United States now in its fifth edition. He has written numerous articles on American history, culture and education. He is married to Mary Quinlivan with whom he shares the proud parentage of four daughters: Christine, Claire, Kathleen, and Julie Ann.